CONTENTS

P9-CAF-547

SPECIAL PULL-OUT CHART

Genesis: an extended outline and reading plan

IN THE BEGINNING

THE NAME OF THE BOOK OF GENESIS

1. *Bereshith* The Jewish name for Genesis, meaning: "In the beginning".
2. *Geneseos* The Septuagint name for Genesis, meaning: Origin, source, generation or beginning.

The word *Geneseos* comes in the Greek Septuagint of 2:4 and 5:1: "The heavens and the earth ... *were created*." "When God *created* man." (The Septuagint, LXX, was a Greek translation of the Old Testament made in the 3rd century BC.)

GENESIS PRESENTS THE BEGINNING OF EVERYTHING – EXCEPT FOR GOD

The beginning of:	Reference in Genesis
the universe	1:1
man and woman	1:27
the Sabbath	2:2-3
marriage	2:22-24
sin	3:1-7
sacrifice and salvation	3:15, 21
the family	4:1-15
civilization	4:16-21
government	9:1-6
nations	11
Israel	12:1-3

Little wonder that the book of Genesis has been called "The book of beginnings."

GENESIS IS GOD-CENTERED

"In the beginning God created
   ... and God said
   ... and God saw
   ... and God blessed
   ... and God finished."

Genesis 1:1, 4, 28, 31; 2:2

OTHER CREATION STORIES
FROM THE ANCIENT NEAR EAST

These stories contrast greatly with the book of Genesis.
There are some superficial similarities: they start in chaos
and end in order. But the differences are far greater:

Ancient Near East stories are:	Genesis in contrast is:
Polytheistic	Monotheistic
Immoral	Ethical
Grotesque	Sublime
Crude	Dignified

GOD IS OUR CREATOR

"In the beginning God ..." depicts the Creator God as full of
wisdom, power, purpose and goodness.

A KEY VERSE
The opening verse of the Bible

"In the beginning God created the heavens and the earth."

Genesis 1:1

KEYS TO UNLOCK GENESIS

KEY WORD
"Beginning."

KEY PHRASE
"In the beginning."

KEY THEME OF GENESIS
God choosing one nation through whom he would bless all
nations. ⌐ creates

KEY SUMMARY: 50 CHAPTERS IN 50 WORDS
"The main purpose of Genesis is the revelation of the
character and purposes of God and of man's fallen state.
In chapters 1–11 we have the beginnings of man's history.
In chapters 12–50 we are told about the beginnings of Israel.
What we are given is virtually only salvation history."
  H.L. Ellison

KEY TO THE START AND THE FINISH OF GENESIS
Genesis starts with life, 1:20-28, and ends with death,
50:26.

"4" IS THE KEY NUMBER
For an overview of one of the longest books in the Bible,
look out for:
• the four major *events* recorded in Genesis
• the four most important *people* featured in Genesis.

FOUR KEY EVENTS		FOUR KEY PEOPLE	
1. Creation	1:1–2:25	1. Abraham	11:10–25:10
2. Fall	3:1–5:32	2. Isaac	25:11–26:35
3. Flood	6:1–9:29	3. Jacob	27:1–36:43
4. Nations	10:1–11:9	4. Joseph	37:1–50:26

KEY FUNDAMENTAL FACTS TAUGHT IN GENESIS

- God exists
- God sustains the world
- Humankind may reject God
- God redeems people
- God acts in history

KEY ANSWERS TO KEY QUESTIONS

• How did our universe begin?	By the action of God
• How did the Israelites come into being?	By God calling them
• What is God like?	• He is the God of creation, the Lord of the whole earth. • He is a good God who looks for goodness. • He is a living God who may be known as a friend.

FACT FILE ON GENESIS

Number of
chapters	verses	words
50	1533	38,267

WHY GENESIS IS THOUGHT OF AS THE "LONGEST" BIBLE BOOK

Genesis covers more time than any other Bible book. In fact, Genesis covers more time than all the other Bible books put together.

WHY GENESIS IS THOUGHT OF AS THE "MOST IMPORTANT" BIBLE BOOK

Genesis is said to be the most important book in the Bible because all the other books are built on it.

Genesis is the indispensable introduction to the entire Bible. The rest of the Bible would make little sense without the book of Genesis.

Genesis is the foundation of all revealed truth. Everything revealed in the other books of the Bible has its beginning in the book of Genesis.

AUTHOR

Traditionally, Moses, is the compiler of the first five books of the Bible.

ARE THEY MOSAIC, OR A MOSAIC?	
Mosaic authorship is supported by a number of inferential evidences:	
• In the Old Testament:	Exodus 24:4
• In the New Testament:	Acts 3:22; 13:39; 15:1; Romans 10:5,19; 1 Corinthians 9:9; 2 Corinthians 3:15
• By Jesus:	Matthew 8:4; 19:7-8; Mark 1:44; 7:10; 10:3-4; Luke 5:14; 16:29,31; John 5:45-46; 7:22-23

A BOOK OF STORIES

Genesis teaches truth through very human stories. There is no covering up the ungodly actions of the people described. Their portraits are painted warts and all.

MAJOR DOCTRINES FIRST MENTIONED IN GENESIS

Evil	Sin	Rebellion
Redemption	Election	Providence
Covenant		

ARCHAEOLOGY CONFIRMS ACCURACY OF GENESIS

1. Near eastern customs

Genesis describes a number of customs which can be paralleled in the records of ancient texts, such as:

the Nuzi texts	15th century BC
the code of Hammurabi	18th century BC
the Mari texts	18th century BC

- A childless man could adopt one of his own male servants to be his heir. This is recorded in the documents uncovered at Nuzi and in Genesis 15:2-4.
- A slave girl being asked to produce an heir when the wife is barren. This ancient custom is illustrated in Old Assyrian marriage contracts, the Code of Hammurabi, the Nuzi tablets and in Genesis 16:2; 30:3-4.

2. Near eastern names

A number of Amorite personal names in these centuries are the same as the Hebrew names recorded in Genesis, such as:

Abram	Jacob
Laban	Zebulun
Benjamin	

3. A Bible event

The Flood Tablets from the *Epic of Gilgamech*, unearthed by H. Rassam in 1855 from Ashurbanipal's library, 669–626 BC, confirm the events described in Genesis 6–9. It is the most striking extra-biblical parallel to any biblical event. It even describes the sending out of the birds from the ship by the Babylonian Noah (Ut-hapistim).

HOW TO READ GENESIS

THE DIVISIONS OF GENESIS

The book of Genesis is divided into twelve sections.
These subject divisions are marked in the Hebrew text by
the word *toledoth* ("generations," or "births"). The King
James Version translates this phrase as "the generations of,"
while the New International Version uses the expression
"the account of." The only exception is the first: Genesis
1:1–2:3.

12 DIVISIONS

1. Creation – the beginning	1:1–2:3
2. The history of the heavens and the earth	2:4–4:26
3. The book of the genealogy of Adam	5:1–6:8
4. The genealogy of Noah	6:9–9:29
5. The genealogy of the sons of Noah	10:1–11:9
6. The genealogy of Shem	11:10-26
7. The genealogy of Terah (Abraham)	11:27–25:11
8. The genealogy of Ishmael	25:12-18
9. The genealogy of Isaac	25:19–35:29
10. The genealogy of Esau	36:1-9
11. The genealogy of the sons of Esau	36:10-43
12. The genealogy of Jacob	37:1–50:26

TWO MAIN SECTIONS

1. From Adam to Abraham, sometimes called "primeval history"	1:1–11:26
2. God's dealings with Abraham, Isaac, Jacob and Joseph, sometimes called "patriarchal history"	11:27–50:26

GENESIS AT A GLANCE

1–11 Primeval history of humanity

1–2   Creation
3   The fall
4–5   From the fall to the flood
6–9   The flood
10–11 From the flood to Abraham

12–50 Patriarchal history of Israel

12–25 Abraham
26–28 Isaac
29–36 Jacob
37–50 Joseph

SEVEN MEN

God used seven men to restore the ruined earth:

Person	Meaning of name	Summary of person
1. Adam	Humankind	First person created by God
2. Abel	Shepherd	God accepted his sacrifice
3. Noah	Comfort	The ark builder
4. Abraham	Father of Many	The spiritual pilgrim
5. Isaac	Laughter	The long-looked-for son
6. Jacob	Supplanter	He lived up to his name
7. Joseph	Increaser	The youth whose dreams came true

CREATION OF THE WORLD

READ FROM GENESIS
1:1–2:3

MAJOR BIBLE STUDY

Compare the verses in Genesis with other Bible references, asking what they reveal about God or our relationship to God. For example, note how Psalm 33:9 confirms Genesis 1:3 and states that the world was made through what God said.

Genesis 1:3	Psalms 33:9; 104:2; Isaiah 45:7; 2 Corinthians 4:6
Genesis 1:4	Psalm 74:16
Genesis 1:7	Job 38:8-11; Psalm 148:4; Proverbs 8:28
Genesis 1:8	Genesis 1:5
Genesis 1:9	Job 26:7; Psalm 95:5; Proverbs 8:29; Jeremiah 5:22; 2 Peter 3:5
Genesis 1:10	Psalms 33:7-8; 95:5
Genesis 1:11	Genesis 2:9; Psalm 104:14; Matthew 6:30
Genesis 1:14	Psalms 74:16; 104:19
Genesis 1:15	Genesis 1:5
Genesis 1:16	Psalms 8:3; 19:1-6; 136:8-9; 1 Corinthians 15:41
Genesis 1:18	Jeremiah 33:20, 25
Genesis 1:20	Genesis 2:19; Psalm 146:6
Genesis 1:21	Psalm 104:25-28
Genesis 1:24	Genesis 2:19
Genesis 1:29	Genesis 9:3; Psalms 104:13; 136:25
Genesis 1:30	Psalms 104:14; 145:15

TEACHING ABOUT GOD

Observe how this passage reveals things about God which we would not have known unless God had revealed them to us.

• **God is the Creator**

The world didn't happen simply by chance. God created it. "In

the beginning God created . . ." *Genesis 1.1*
- **Everything in creation was made by God**
  "Through him all things were made; without him nothing was made that has been made." *John 1:3*
- **Everything that God made was good**
  "God saw all that he had made, and it was very good." *Genesis 1:31*
- **Humans are different from all other creatures**
  a. Only humans are made in God's likeness
  "Then God said, 'Let us make man in our image, in our likeness." *Genesis 1:26*
  b. Humans are to be in charge of all the other creatures
  "Let them rule over the fish of the sea and the birds of the air, over the livestock, over the earth, and over all the creatures that move along the ground." *Genesis 1:26*
- **On the seventh day God rested from all his work**
  The idea of one rest day in seven is not just in the Ten Commandments, but is a basic instruction of our Maker.
  "God ... rested from all his work. And God blessed the seventh day and made it holy." *Genesis 2:3*

MADE IN GOD'S IMAGE

"In the Old Testament the two Hebrew words translated 'likeness' and 'image' have the same meaning. They reveal that human beings, as distinct from animals, were "created to be in a special relationship with God ... personal and eternal." *George Carey, Archbishop of Canterbury*

Since all men and women and children are in God's likeness, they are to be treated with respect.

GOD'S ORDER IN CREATION
At God's command the world came into being.
Follow the phrase, "And God said", which occurs eight times in the first chapter of Genesis.

Day 1	Light and darkness
Day 2	The sky
Day 3	Earth with plants and trees, the sea
Day 4	Sun, moon and stars
Day 5	Birds and fish
Day 6	Animals and man

CREATION OR EVOLUTION?

TRY NOT TO ARGUE ABOUT GENESIS

Derek Kidner, one of the most helpful Bible commentators on the book of Genesis, has written: "There can scarcely be another part of Scripture over which so many battles, theological, scientific, historical and literary, have been fought, or so many strong opinions cherished."

THE BIBLE AND SCIENCE

1. For every argument that is used to question the accuracy of the book of Genesis, there are more historical and scientific arguments which support it.

2. Genesis is truth made known by God. Genesis can equally be understood by a 1st century person and a 21st century person, by a young person and by a scientific person. What other writing can be understood by a child and yet baffle a scholar?

GO TO GENESIS FOR THEOLOGY

Moses' primary purpose in writing the book of Genesis was to tell us about God and what God has done for us. This means that some things that linguists, scientists, sociologists and psychologists look for may not be found in Genesis.

The Bible is first and foremost a book about salvation.

FREQUENTLY ASKED QUESTIONS ABOUT GENESIS CHAPTER 1

1. Can a Christian believe in any form of evolution?

"I cannot see that at least some forms of the theory of evolution contradict or are contradicted by the Genesis revelation. Scripture reveals religious truths about God, that his creative program culminated in man; science suggests that 'evolution' may have been the mode which God employed in creating.

"I recognize, however, that other Clrristians who accept and uphold the authority of Scripture reject the theory of evolution as being (in their view) incompatible with biblical teaching.

"As the debate continues, it is particularly important for all of us (whichever position we hold) to try to:
• distinguish both between scientific fact and scientific theory, …

• distinguish between what the Bible plainly asserts and what we may like to think it asserts."
John Stott

2. Was Adam the first man?

Most Christians are firm in their belief that Adam and Eve were historical people. They rule out the possibility that there were other human types before Adam. Astoundingly. a handful of religious leaders argue that there may have been pre-Adamic people often referred to by scientists as *homo erectus*.

When Genesis 1:27 says "God created man in his own image", it is referring to the first complete man, the first person to bear the image of God. This first person, Adam, couild have been called *homo divinus*!

FAITH

"By *faith* we understand that the universe was formed at God's command, so that what is seen was not made out of what was visible." *Hebrews 11:3*

FALL OF HUMANKIND

READ FROM GENESIS
3:1-24

ADAM'S FALL

a. Commandment *given*: "You must not eat from the tree." *2:17*

b. Commandment *questioned*: "Did God really say …?" *3:1*

c. Commandment *denied*: "You will not surely die." *3:4*

d. Commandment *disobeyed*: "And he ate it." *3:6*

EVE'S FALL

"When the woman saw that the fruit of the tree was good for food and pleasing to the eye, and also desirable for gaining wisdom, she took some and ate it." *3:6*

a. Eve *saw* the fruit

b. Eve *desired* the fruit

c. Eve *took* the fruit

SATAN'S TACTICS

His cunning employed in Genesis 3 continues to be used today to bring about humankind's fall.

• Doubt: doubt makes us question God's Word and his goodness.

• Desire: Adam and Eve were motivated by greed and the desire to gain wisdom.

• Doing: with doubt in their minds they acted on their desire and sinned.

RESULTS OF REBELLION

• Companionship lost 3:8

• Guilt 3:7

• Fear 3:10

• Refusal to accept personal responsibility:
  Adam implied it was Eve's and God's fault. *12*
  Eve implied it was the serpent's fault. *13*

18

MINI BIBLE STUDY
1. Read Hebrews 11:5 to see how Enoch is commended as a man of faith in God.
2. Read 2 Kings 2:10 about the only other person in the Bible who did not die.

STUDY A THEME IN GENESIS
1. WHAT GOD TEACHES IN GENESIS

1. TEACHING ABOUT GOD

God has life in himself and is eternal	*1.1*
God is the life-giver and creator	*1:1–2:9*
God is personal and wishes to have a personal relationship with us	*1:26–2:25; 3:8*
God is holy. God will judge sinful humankind	*3:8-24; 6:5-8; 11:1-9; 18:16–19:29*
God is merciful	*3:21; 4:15; 6:8; 18:32*
God is sovereign	*18:14; 26:12-16*

2. TEACHING ABOUT HUMANKIND

We are born in the image of God	*1:27-30*
We go our own way and sin against God	*3:1-7*

3. TEACHING ABOUT SOCIETY

We were not created as isolated individuals, but as social beings. "The Lord God said, 'It is not good for the man to be alone. I will make a helper suitable for him.'"	*2:18*
Marriage is the basic structure of society.	*2:24*

4. FOUR KEY THEMES IN GENESIS

a. SALVATION
As soon as Adam, the very first human, sinned, God showed he had a rescue plan to save not only him but all of humankind. Genesis 3:15, 4:4, and 22:8 point to what Jesus would one day accomplish for us.

b. WORK
It was only after the fall that the gift of work, *1:28*, turned into toil, *3:17-19*.

c. SATAN
His activity is clearly seen in the original fall, *3:1-7*.

d. WORSHIP
Faith, a loving response of obedience and trust, is an indispensable requirement in order for a person to worship God, *4:1-7*.

22

23

WHY THE FLOOD?

READ FROM GENESIS
6:1-22

WHAT THE STORY OF NOAH ILLUSTRATES

Noah's rescue from the flood foreshadows God's redemption of his followers.

- "God... did not spare the ancient world when he brought the flood on its ungodly people, but protected Noah, a preacher of righteousness, and seven others." *2 Peter 2:5*
- "By faith Noah, when warned about things not yet seen, in holy fear built an ark to save his family. By his faith he condemned the world and became heir of the righteousness that comes by faith." *Hebrews 11:7*

TYPES OF CHRIST IN GENESIS

Types: A "type" is an historical fact that illustrates a spiritual truth.

NOAH AS A TYPE OF JESUS

Noah's godly qualities are seen as a type of Jesus, even though Noah was not always perfect.

Examples	in Genesis	compare with
Noah pleased God	6:8-9	Matthew 3:17; John 8:29
God's will is revealed to him	6:13-22	John 17:4,8
Prepared the way of salvation	6:14	Hebrews 11:7; Romans 5:6,8; John 14:6
Finished God's work	6:22	John 17:4; 19:30

"Noah did everything just as God commanded him." *Genesis 6:22*

"I have brought you glory on earth by completing the work you gave me to do." *John 17:4*

"When he had received the drink, Jesus said, 'It is finished.' With that, he bowed his head and gave up his spirit." *John 19:30*

24

A KEY VERSE
Depraved humankind
"The Lord saw how great man's wickedness on the earth had become, and that every inclination of the thoughts of his heart was only evil all the time." *6:5*

God's deep grief
"The Lord was grieved that he had made man on earth, and his heart was full of pain." *6:6*

NOAH – AN EXAMPLE TO US

1. He walked with God in the middle of evil	*6:8-12*
2. He was obedient when given a hard task	*6:14,22; 7:5*

"Noah was the first of many individuals who, apparently single-handed, have been used by God to carry out his purpose and to make a crucial difference to the world ...

"Even today people famous and people unknown are making a difference in the world simply by trying to obey God ...

"They have refused to be bullied into believing that what they do makes no difference." *Stephen Travis*

3. He lived by faith as he built the ark.	*Hebrews 11:7*
4. He warned his neighbors about the impending flood.	*2 Peter 2:5*

THE FLOOD ITSELF

READ FROM GENESIS
7:1 - 8:19

GOD'S COMMANDS
1. The last command Noah received from God before the ark was shut:
"Go into the ark." *7:1*
2. The first command Noah received from God after the flood:
"Come out of the ark." *8:16*

"THE LORD SHUT HIM IN" *7:16*
This heralded two things:
1. Judgment for the rest of humankind
2. Protection for Noah and his family

"GOD REMEMBERED NOAH" *8:1*
- Noah had not heard from God for 150 days. *7:24*
- But God had not forgotten Noah and those with him.
- When God "remembers" us, he shows his care for us.

MINI BIBLE STUDY

How do the cross references shed light on the verses from Genesis 8?

Verse in Genesis 8	Compare with cross reference/s
Genesis 8:1 "But God remembered Noah and all the wild animals and the livestock that were with him in the ark, and he sent a wind over the earth, and the waters receded."	Genesis 19:29; 30:22; Exodus 2:24; 14:21; Isaiah 44:27
Genesis 8:1	Then Moses stretched out his hand over the sea, and all that night the Lord drove back with a strong east wind and turned it into dry land." *Exodus 14:21* "Who says to the watery deep, 'Be dry, and I will dry up your streams.'" *Isaiah 44:27*
Genesis 8:7	Leviticus 11:15; 1 Kings 17:4; Luke 12:24
Genesis 8:8	Isaiah 60:8; Hosea 11:11; Matthew 10:16

STUDY A THEME IN GENESIS
2. PROPHECIES IN GENESIS

PROPHECIES ABOUT JESUS

Prophesied in Genesis		Fulfilled in Jesus
1. The "offspring of the woman" [Eve] *3:15*	Offspring of a woman	"But when the time had fully come, God sent his Son, born of a woman, born under law." *Galatians 4:4*
2. "Abraham will surely become a great and powerful nation, and all nations on earth will be blessed through him." *18:18*	Promised offspring of Abraham	"And you are heirs of the prophets and of the covenant God made with your fathers. He said to Abraham, Through your offspring all peoples on earth will be blessed.'" *Acts 3:25*

ISRAEL WILL GO TO EGYPT
1. Prophecy
"Then the Lord said to him, 'Know for certain that your descendants will be strangers in a country not their own, and they will be enslaved and ill-treated four hundred years. But I will punish the nation they serve as slaves, and afterwards they will come out with great possessions." *Genesis 15:13-14*

2. Details of fulfilment of prophecy

Prophecy	Fulfilment
a. Enslaved	
"… and they will be enslaved …"	"So they put slave masters over them to oppress them with forced labor, and they built Pithom and Rameses as store cities for Pharaoh." *Exodus 1:11*
b. Length of stay in Egypt	
"…and ill-treated four hundred years." ["400" here is a round number.]	"Now the length of time the Israelite people lived in Egypt was 430 years." *Exodus 14:20*
c. Promise of deliverance	
"But I will punish the nation they serve as slaves, and afterwards they will come out …"	"Therefore say to the Israelites: 'I am the Lord, and I will bring you out from under the yoke of the Egyptians. I will free you from being slaves to them." *Exodus 6:6* "Pharaoh let the people go." *Exodus 13:17*
d. Will not leave empty-handed	
"… they will come out with great possessions."	"The Israelites did as Moses instructed and asked the Egyptians for articles of silver and gold and for clothing. The Lord made them favorably disposed towards the people, and they gave them what they asked for; so they plundered the Egyptians." *Exodus 12:35-36*

THE KINGSHIP OF JESUS
1. Prophesied
"The scepter will not depart from Judah, nor the ruler's staff from between his feet, until he comes to whom it belongs and the obedience of the nations is his." *49:10*

2. Fulfilled
"Where is the one who has been born king of the Jews?" *Matthew 2:2*

A NEW BEGINNING

READ FROM GENESIS
8:20–9:29

THE RAINBOW

1. Meaning of the rainbow
"I have set my rainbow in the clouds, and it will be the sign of the covenant between me and the earth." *9:13*

2. The first rainbow?
Whether rain and rainbows existed before Noah and the flood we're not certain. Certain scholars believe this was the first occurrence of rain and a rainbow. But after the flood the rainbow was given a specific meaning by God. It became the sign of God's covenant with Noah and his descendants.

3. An example of God's mercy
God showed his mercy to Noah and his family and to all subsequent generations in his covenant.
"As long as the earth endures, seedtime and harvest, cold and heat, summer and winter, day and night will never cease." *8:22*

OTHER RAINBOWS IN THE BIBLE

1. The rainbow in Ezekiel

"Above the expanse over their heads was what looked like a throne of sapphire, and high above on the throne was a figure like that of a man. I saw that from what appeared to be his waist up he looked like glowing metal, as if full of fire, and that from there down he looked like fire; and brilliant light surrounded him. Like the appearance of a rainbow in the clouds on a rainy day, so was the radiance around him." *Ezekiel 1:26-28a*

Ezekiel's interpretation of the rainbow

"This was the appearance of the likeness of the glory of the Lord." *Ezekiel 1:28b*

Ezekiel's response on seeing the rainbow

"When I saw it, I fell face down, and I heard the voice of one speaking." *Ezekiel 1:28c*

2. The rainbow in Revelation

"At once I was in the Spirit, and there before me was a throne in heaven with someone sitting on it. And the one who sat there had the appearance of jasper and camelian. A rainbow, resembling an emerald, encircled the throne." *Revelation 4:2-3*

This rainbow speaks of God's majesty.

God's covenant was his unconditional promise never again to destroy all the earth. There still will be natural disasters, but they will not be worldwide, and they may therefore be overcome.

THE NATIONS SPREAD

READ FROM GENESIS
10:1–11:26

NOAH'S THREE SONS

"This is the account of Shem, Ham and Japheth, Noah's sons, who themselves had sons after the flood." *10:1*

1. Shem

The descendants of Shem were called "Shemites" and, later on, "Semites." *10:21-31*. Abraham, and the Jewish and Arab nations, descend from the line of Shem.

2. Ham

The descendants of Ham, the Hamites, were located in south-west Asia and north-east Africa. *10:6-20*

3. Japheth

The 14 nations that came from Japheth, *10:2-5* plus the 30 from Ham and Shem's 26, *10:2-3* add up to 70 nations.

The numbers "7" and "10" both symbolize completeness in the Bible.

THE TOWER OF BABEL AND GOD'S JUDGMENT ON HUMAN PRIDE *11:1-9*

The tower of Babel

This tower may have been a ziggurat. These temple-towers were constructed of brick in the shape of a terraced pyramid and set on an artificial mound. Ziggurats were being built in Babylonia as early as 3,000 B.C.

The purpose of the Tower of Babel

The idea was to gain fame, power and domination. It was a take-over bid and would have had dire results for the world. *11:6*

The results of building the tower of Babel

1. It resulted in the confusion of languages
"That is why it was called Babel – because there the Lord confused the language of the whole world. *11:9*

2. It resulted in the scattering of the nations.
"From there the Lord scattered them over the face of the whole earth." *11:9*

ABRAHAM: HIS CALL

📖 **READ FROM GENESIS**
12–14

FACT FILE: **ABRAHAM**

Born:	Ur of the Chaldeans, in Mesopotarnia (Iraq)
Date:	Probably around 1,900 B.C.
Called by God:	To leave Haran and go to an unspecified country
Lived:	Most of his life south of Canaan
Occupation:	Wealthy livestock owner and trader
Relatives:	Brothers: Nahor and Haran Father: Terah Wife: Sarah Nephew: Lot
Children:	Two sons: Ishmael and Isaac
Contemporaries:	Abimelech, Melchizedek
Died:	Age 175
Buried:	In the family burying-place at Machpelah *Gen. 25:7-10*

GOD'S SEVENFOLD PROMISE TO ABRAHAM

1. "I will make you a great nation."
2. "I will bless you."
3. "I will make your name great."
4. "You will be a blessing."
5. "I will bless those who bless you."
6. "Whoever curses you I will curse."
7. "All peoples on earth will be blessed through you." *12:2-3*

ABRAHAM'S STRENGTHS AND ACCOMPLISHMENTS

- In spite of the risk, he obeyed God's call.
- His faith pleased God.
- He was the founder of the Jewish and Arab nations.
- He was not power-seeking or greedy, chapter 13.
- Fully aware of the consequences and danger he set off at the head of a small army to rescue Lot, chapter 14.
- His life was characterized by prayer.

ABRAHAM'S WEAKNESS

He lied by saying Sara (his wife) was his sister, to save his own skin. A disgusted Pharaoh had him expelled from Egypt. *12:10-20.*

ABRAHAM'S LIFE SUMMARIZED IN THE NEW TESTAMENT

He is called:
- "God's friend" *James 2:23*
- "Man of faith" *Galatians 3:9*
- "The father of us all" *Romans 4:16*

Abraham entered upon the adventure of obedience, taking his part in God's salvation plan for the world. This is an adventure open to all Christians.

A KEY VERSE

"Abraham believed the Lord, and he credited it to him as righteousness." *Genesis 15.6*

MINI BIBLESTUDY

Abraham's story is told in Genesis 11–25.

He is also mentioned in:
- Exodus 2:24
- Acts 7:2-8
- Romans 4
- Galatians 3
- Hebrews 2:16; 6:13-16; 7:1-10

GOD'S COVENANT

READ FROM GENESIS
15–17

ABRAHAM'S VISION
"Do not be afraid, Abram. I am your shield, your very great reward." *15:1*

LOOK AT THE SKY
To an old, childless man, the Lord said: "'Look up at the heavens and count the stars – if indeed you can count them.' Then he said to him, 'so shall your offspring be.'" *15:5*

HOW MANY STARS DID ABRAHAM SEE?
On a clear night more than 8,000 stars can be seen in the Near-Eastern sky. Abraham believed that God could do this seemingly impossible thing.

ABRAHAM BELIEVED
Abraham changed from doubt and despair (*15:2,3*) to hope and trust. Abram was Abraham's name before he was called Abraham.

"Abram believed the Lord, and he credited to him as righteousness." *15:6*

The rest of the Old Testament and all the New Testament are an outworking of the promises God made to Abraham. Abraham's faith was not a human achievement which he arrived at on his own. It was a response to God's grace.

OUTWORKING OF THESE PROMISES

Old Testament:	Israel was the promised offspring
New Testament:	Christians are Abraham's offspring: "If you belong to Christ, then you are Abraham's seed." *Galatians 3:29*
Final fulfilment:	In heaven Abraham's offspring are: "A great multitude that no one could count." *Revelation 7:9*

THE SIGN OF THE COVENANT

God appointed circumcision to be the sign of the covenant, or agreement made between God and Abraham, *15:8-21*.

"You are to undergo circumcision, and it will be the sign of the covenant between you and me." *17:11*

EIGHT DAYS OLD

"For the generations to come every male among you who is eight days old must be circumcised." *17:12*

In the New Testament we read of:

John the Baptist
"On the eighth day they came to circumcise the child ..." *Luke 1.59*

Jesus
"On the eighth day, when it was time to circumcise him, he was named Jesus." *Luke 2:21*

Paul
"If anyone else thinks he has reasons to put confidence in the flesh, I have more: circumcised on the eighth day ..." *Philippians 3:4-5*

MINI BIBLE STUDY

What did circumcision signify?
• Leviticus 26:41
• Deuteronomy 10:16
• Jeremiah 4:4
• Romans 2:20
• 1 Corinthians 7:19

While it is true that other nations practiced circumcision, *see Jeremiah 9:25-26*, none of them did so as a sign of keeping God's covenant.

STUDY A THEME IN GENESIS
3. COVENANTS

JESUS AND THE NEW COVENANT
The background to Jesus' words, "This cup is the new covenant in my blood …" *Luke 22:20*, is the teaching about the covenant in the Old Testament.

UNCONDITIONAL COVENANT MADE WITH NOAH
Genesis 9:8-17
The covenant was made with "righteous" Noah and his descendants and with every living creature on earth.
Sign of this covenant: rainbow in the storm cloud *9:13*

COVENANT MADE WITH ABRAHAM
1. Genesis 12:1-3
God initiated this covenant with Abraham promising land, descendants, and a blessing.

2. Genesis 13:14-17
After Lot separated from Abraham, God again promised land to Abraham and his descendants.

COVENANT MADE WITH ABRAHAM CONTINUED
1. Genesis 15:1-21
The covenant was ratified when God passed between the sacrificial animals with a smoking firepot and a blazing torch.

2. Genesis 17:1-27
When Abram was 99, God renewed his covenant: changing Abram's name to Abraham (father of a multitude), and initiating circumcision as the sign of the covenant.

The covenant "sign" was a visible seal and reminder of the commitments to the covenant made by God and Abraham.

3. Genesis 22:15-18
God confirms the covenant and emphasizes Abraham's obedience. The covenant made with Abraham was conditional – because it required obedience.

MINI BIBLE STUDY
Other covenants in the Old Testament

1. Covenant at Sinai *(See Exodus 19-24)*
Conditional promise to be Israel's God; Israel to live by his laws.

2. Covenant with Phineas *(See Numbers 25:10-31)*
Unconditional promise to give the family of Phineas a priesthood forever.

3. Covenant with David *(See 2 Samuel 7:5-16)*
Unconditional promise to give Israel a king like David.

A KEY VERSE
The *new* covenant

"'The time is coming,' declares the Lord, 'when I will make a new covenant with the house of Israel and with the house of Judah.'"
Jeremiah 31:31

Jeremiah 31:31-34 is the longest sequence of Old Testament verses to be quoted in their entirety in the New Testament.
See Hebrews 8:8-12.

TESTING THE COVENANT

READ FROM GENESIS
18:1–25:18

READING THROUGH 18:1–25:18
What to look for

Testing the covenant	18:1–20:18
Sarah's faith is tested	18:1-15
Abraham's faith is tested	18:16-33
Sodom and Gomorrah are destroyed	19:1-29
Lot's sin	19:30-38
Abimelech is tested	20:1-18
Consummation of the covenant	**21:1–25:18**
Isaac's birth	21:1-34
Offering Isaac	22:1-24
Death of Sarah	23:1-20
Isaac's marriage	24:1-67
Death of Abraham	25:1-18

Ask a question
As you read each chapter, ask this question of the passage: What does it teach about God?

What does chapter 18 teach about God?
Nothing is too hard for God. "Is anything too hard for the Lord?" the Lord asked Abraham. *18:14*

What does chapter 19 teach about God?
God does not tolerate flagrant sin.

"[The Lord] overthrew those cities [Sodom and Gomorrah]." *19:25*

What does chapter 20 teach about God?
God is a God of healing. "God healed Abimelech." *20:17*

What does chapter 21 teach about God?
God keeps his promises. "The Lord did for Sarah what he had promised." *21:1*

What does chapter 22 teach about God?

God tests us, in order to increase our faith.

"God tested Abraham." *22:1*

What does chapter 23 teach about God?

God blesses the continuing faith of Abraham. Abraham's purchase of the land was an act of faith showing his determination that his family stay in the land.

"Abraham buried his wife Sarah in the care in the field of Machpelah." *23:19*

What does chapter 24 teach about God?

God guides us in answer to prayer.

"Before I finished praying in my heart, Rebekah came out." *24:45*

What does chapter 25 teach about God?

God blesses his followers.

"After Abraham's death, God blessed his son Isaac." *25:11*

MINI BIBLE STUDY

41

Note how God often used dreams to reveal his will. Genesis 28:12; 31:10-11; 37:5-9; 40:5; 41:1.

TYPES OF CHRIST IN GENESIS
The ram as a type of Jesus

Abraham said to Isaac:

"God himself will provide the lamb ..." *22:8*

Just as Abraham drew his knife to kill his son Isaac for a sacrifice God provided.

"Abraham looked up and there in a thicket he saw a ram caught by its horns. He went over and took the ram and sacrificed it as a burnt offering instead of his son." *22:13*

The ram was sacrificed in the place of Isaac.

Jesus was sacrificed in our place.

"We have been made holy through the sacrifice of the body of Jesus Christ once for all." *Hebrews 10:10*

LIFE OF ISAAC

READ FROM GENESIS
25:19–26:35

IN SUMMARY

- Isaac was the long-awaited son whom God had promised to Abraham and Sarah.
- Isaac and his wife, Rebekah, had twin sons – Esau and Jacob.
- In Isaac's old age, he was tricked into blessing Jacob with the blessing he had reserved for Esau.

ISAAC'S CHARACTERISTICS

- He was submissive to his father.
  "Abraham took the wood for the burnt offering and placed it on his son Isaac." *22:6*

- He meditated.
  "He went out to the field one evening to meditate." *24:63*

- He was affectionate
  "He married Rebekah... and he loved her." *24:67*

- He sinned in the same way Abraham had. *See Genesis 12:13.*
  "When the men of that place asked him about his wife, he said, 'she is my sister,' because he was afraid to say, 'she is my wife.' He thought, 'The men of this place might kill me on account of Rebekah, because she is beautiful.'" *26:7*

- He sought to make peace when there was a quarrel.
  The herdsmen of Gerar had twice quarreled with Isaac's herdsmen over wells, so Isaac, "moved on ... and dug another well, and no one quarrelled over it." *26:22*

- He was prayerful.
  "Isaac built an altar there and called on the name of the Lord." *26:25*

- He was a man of faith.
  "By faith Isaac blessed Jacob and Esau in regard to their future." *Hebrews 11:20*

- He was obedient to God.
  "Now there was a famine in the land. ... The Lord appeared to Isaac and said, 'Do not go down to Egypt.' ... So Isaac stayed in Gerar." *26:1,6*

MINI BIBLE STUDY

The Bible often says that God sustains and protects his people. "Stay in this land for a while, and I will be with you and will bless you." *26:3*

Some other verses to look up on the same theme are:

Genesis	Joshua	Isaiah	Jeremiah	Matthew	Acts
26:24	1:5	41:10	1:8	28:20	18:9-10
28:15			1:19		
31:3					

Are these promises conditional? If so, on what?

STUDY A THEME IN GENESIS
4. GENESIS IN THE NEW TESTAMENT

THE BIBLE AND THE HOLY SPIRIT
"The sacred books are pervaded by the fulness of the Spirit. There is nothing either in the prophets, or the law, or the gospels, or in the letters, which does not spring from the fulness of the divine majesty." *Origen*

LINKS BETWEEN GENESIS AND THE REST OF THE BIBLE
The book of Genesis provides the foundation for the rest of the Bible with its history and theology. It is surprising to see how many things written about in Genesis are referenced in the New Testament. Sometimes more details are given in the New Testament. This is clear in the case of Abel.

Topic in Genesis	References in Genesis	Linked Bible references
1. Creation "In the beginning God created the heavens and the earth."	1:1	John 1:3; Hebrews 11:3 "Through him all things were made; without him nothing was made that has been made." "By faith we understand that the universe was formed at God's command, so that what is seen was not made out of what is visible."
2. Marriage and divorce	1:27; 2:23,24	Matthew 19:4-6
3. Deception of Eve	3:1-4	2 Corinthians 11:3
		1 Timothy 2:14
4. Adam's disobedience	3:6	Romans 5:12-14
5. Promised Messiah	3:15	Galatians 4:4-5
6. Abel's offering accepted	4:4	Hebrews 11:4
7. Cain's evil actions	4:3-16	Jude 11

HEBREWS 11

Hebrews 11:1-22 gives the best summary of the people of faith who are found in the fifty chapters of Genesis.

8. Translation of Enoch "Enoch walked with God; then he was no more, because God took him away."	5:24	Hebrews 11:5 "By faith Enoch was taken from this life, so that he did not experience death; he could not be found, because God had taken him away."
9. Deliverance of Noah	6:18	1 Peter 3:20
10. Noah preparing the ark	6:14-22	Hebrews 11:7
11. The flood	6:11-13;7:4	Matthew 24:37-39
12. Call of Abraham	12:1	Hebrews 11:8
13. Melchizedek's priesthood	14:18-20	Hebrews 5:6; 7:1
14. Abraham's faith	15:6	Romans 4:3; James 2:23
15. Hagar and Ishmael	16:15	Galatians 4:22
16. Days of Lot	19:1-29	Luke 17:28-29
17. Destruction of Sodom and Gomorrah	19:25	Matthew 10:15; 11:23-24
18. Lot's wife "But Lot's wife looked back, and she became a pillar of salt."	19:26	Luke 17:32 "Remember Lot's wife!" *Luke 17:32*
19. Offering of Isaac	22:1-14	Hebrews 11:17; James 2:21
20. Joseph's dying request	50:24,25	Hebrews 11:22

LIFE OF JACOB (A)

📖 **READ FROM GENESIS**
27:1–31:55

FACT FILE: **JACOB**

Meaning of name:	"Supplanter," figuratively, "he deceives"
Occupation:	Shepherd, livestock owner
Relatives:	Parents: Isaac and Rebekah Twin brother: Esau Father-in-law: Laban Wives: Rachel and Leah
Children:	His twelve sons are founders of the twelve tribes of Israel
Strengths:	Determined, willing to work long and hard for what he wanted Good businessman
Weaknesses:	When faced with conflict, relies on his own resources rather than going to God for help and resorts to shady practices Tends to accumulate wealth for its own sake Indulges one favorite son causing jealousy and dissension

46

TYPES OF CHRIST IN GENESIS
Note on Jacob's "ladder" to heaven
Jacob's dream at Bethel:
Genesis 28:10-22
Jacob's so-called "ladder" was more like a stairway.

JACOB'S "LADDER" AS A TYPE OF CHRIST
"He [Jacob] had a dream in which he saw a stairway resting on the earth, with its top reaching to heaven, and the angels of God were ascending and descending on it." *28:12*

The words "the angels of God were ascending and descending on it" indicate that the Lord offered to be Jacob's God.

A KEY VERSE

"I am with you and will watch over you wherever you go, and I will bring you back to this land. I will not leave you until I have done what I have promised you." *28:15*

JACOB'S "LADDER" LINKED TO JESUS

1. "He [Jesus] then added [speaking to one of his disciples, Nathanael], 'I tell you the truth, you shall see heaven open, and the angels of God ascending and descending on the Son of Man.'" *John 1.51*

2. Jesus said he was the bridge between heaven and earth. "I am the way and the truth and the life. No one comes to the Father except through me." *John 14:6*

3. Jesus is the only "mediator between God and men." *1 Timothy 2:5*

LIFE OF JACOB (B)

READ FROM GENESIS
32:3–36:4

TYPES OF CHRIST IN GENESIS
Jacob, as a man of prayer
Compare Genesis 32.22-32 with John 11:41-42 and John 17:1-26.

JACOB'S WRESTLING WITH GOD: GENESIS 32:22-32
"Then the man said, 'Your name will no longer be Jacob, but Israel, because you have struggled with God and with men and have overcome.'" *32:28*

CHANGE OF NAME
"Your name will no longer be Jacob."
As he is about to enter the promised land, Jacob acknowledges that he is dependent on God who is the source of blessing. Now by changing Jacob's name, the Lord acknowledges that Jacob is his servant.

JACOB/ISRAEL
In "Jacob/Israel" the nation of Israel received her name and one of her abiding characteristics.
• The people who struggle with God is commemorated in the name Israel. "Israel" means "he struggles with God."
• The people who struggle with men is commemorated in the name Jacob.

MINI BIBLE STUDY
Key passages about Jacob outside Genesis

Hosea 12:2-6	Like Jacob, the people had to return to God.
Romans 9:11-13	God's choice is not dependent on our goodness.
Hebrews 11:9, 20-21	Jacob's growing faith.

TWO KEY VERSES

"And God said to him [Jacob], 'I am God Almighty; be fruitful and increase in number. A nation and a community of nations will come from you, and kings will come from your body. The land I gave to Abraham and Isaac I also give to you, and I will give this land to your descendants after you.'" *35:11-12*

• God confirms to Jacob the same covenant promises which he had made to Abraham. *See Genesis 17:1-8.*

• These words reflect God's original blessing given to humankind at creation. "God blessed them and said to them, 'Be fruitful and increase in number; fill the earth and subdue it. Rule over the fish of the sea and the birds of the air and over every living creature that moves on the ground.'" *1:28*

• These words were also renewed after the flood.
"Then God blessed Noah and his sons, saying to them, 'Be fruitful and increase in number and fill the earth.'" *9:1*

• God tells Jacob that his blessing on humankind will be fulfilled through Jacob and his descendants.
"Now the Israelites settled in Egypt in the region of Goshen. They acquired property there and were fruitful and increased greatly in number." *47:27*

LIFE OF JACOB (C)

READ FROM GENESIS
33:1–36:43

THE LIFE OF JACOB

Jacob, the deceiver, was transformed by God into Israel, the prince of God. The following guide shows how this cheater became one of the patriarchs and a man noted for his faith in God.

JACOB'S EARLY LIFE

1. He cheats his brother Esau out of his birthright – the inheritance rights due to the firstborn. *25:29-34*
2. He deceives his elderly father and receives the blessing instead of Esau. *27:1-29*
3. He flees for his life. He is told to find a wife in Haran. *27:41; 28:1-5*

JACOB IN HARAN

1. Jacob is deceived by Laban into marrying Leah. *29:15-30*
2. Jacob and Laban have a quarrelsome disagreement. *30:1-43*
3. God tells Jacob to return to the promised land. *31:3* "Then the Lord said to Jacob, 'Go back to the land of your fathers and to your relatives, and I will be with you.'" *31:3*
4. Jacob is met by angelic messengers. *32:1-2*

50

A KEY VERSE

"By faith Jacob, when he was dying, blessed each of Joseph's sons, and worshiped as he leaned on the top of his staff" *Hebrews 11:21*

JACOB'S GREAT SPIRITUAL STRUGGLE

1. Jacob turns to prayer as he prepares to face Esau's four hundred men. *32:3-12*
2. Jacob wrestles all night with God. *32:24-32*
3. Jacob has a happy meeting with Esau. *33:1-16*
4. Jacob's daughter Dinah is defiled. *34:1-5*
5. The trouble brought by his sons' revenge. *34:7-31*
6. Jacob builds an altar at Bethel. *35:1-15*

JACOB'S LATER YEARS

1. Parental favoritism and the brothers' jealousy lead to Joseph being sold into slavery. *37:1-36*
2. More family troubles arise – Judah and Tamar. *38:1-30*
3. On his deathbed, Jacob blesses his sons and grandsons. *48:1–49:33*

MOUNTAIN-TOP EXPERIENCES IN GENESIS

1. Ararat

Ararat is a range of mountains in modern-day Turkey.

"On the seventeenth day of the seventh month the ark came to rest on the mountains of Ararat." *8:4*

• Ararat signaled a new beginning
• Ararat has been called "the patriarch of mountains"
• Ararat smoked with the first sacrifice of the restored world, *8:20-21*
• Ararat and an instructive New Testament cross-reference: *Romans 12:1-2*

2. Moriah

Genesis 22:2-14

Later, Moriah became the site of the Jerusalem temple.

"Then God said, 'Take your son, your only son, Isaac, whom you love, and go to the region of Moriah. Sacrifice him there as a burnt offering on one of the mountains I will tell you about." *22:2*

• Moriah, the mount of testing
• Moriah and the victory of faith
• Moriah, called by Abraham, "The Lord Will Provide." *22:14*
• Moriah and instructive New Testament cross-references: *1 Peter 4:12-14; Philippians 4.19*

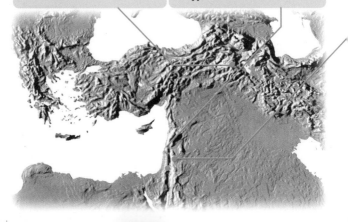

3. Gilead

Genesis 31:25,42-52

Gilead is to the south-east of Lake Galilee.

"Jacob pitched his tent in the hill country of Gilead when Laban overtook him, and Laban and his relatives camped there too." *31:25*

- Gilead, the mount of disunity
- Gilead and quarrels among brethren
- Gilead, the place where quarrels were made up
- Gilead and its pillar of stones

a. Laban's name for the pillar of stones:

"Laban called it Jegar Sahadutha." *31:47*

In Aramaic, "Jegar Sahadutha" means "witness heap".

b. Jacob's name for the pillar of stones:

"And Jacob called it Galeed." *31:47*

In Hebrew, "Galeed" means "witness heap".

"Laban said, 'This heap is a witness between you and me today.' That is why it was called Galeed. It was also called Mizpah, because he said, 'May the Lord keep watch between you and me when we are away from each other.'" *31:49*

OTHER IMPORTANT MOUNTAINS IN THE BIBLE

Sinai/Horeb	God gives the Ten Commandments	*Exodus 19:20*
	Elijah hears God's still small voice	*1 Kings 19:7-18*
Carmel	Elijah's decisive confrontation with the priests of Baal	*1 Kings 18:20-45*
Hermon	Probable site of the Transfiguration of Jesus	*Matthew 17:1-8*
Calvary	The site of Jesus' crucifixion	*Luke 23:33*

LIFE OF JOSEPH (A)

READ FROM GENESIS
37:1-38:30

READ THROUGH THE WHOLE JOSEPH STORY

What strikes you in this story:
- Is it Joseph?
- Is it his brothers?
- Is it his father?
- Is it God's providential care?

1. Joseph's dreams and their sequel	37:1-36
2. Judah's family	38:1-30
3. Potiphar's wife	39:1-23
4. Joseph in prison	40:1-23
5. Pharaoh's dreams	41:1-36
6. Joseph's rise to power	41:37-57
7. The brothers' first visit to Egypt	42:1-38
8. The brothers' second visit to Egypt	43:1-34
9. The final testing	44:1-34
10. Joseph makes himself known	45:1-28
11. Jacob goes to Egypt	46:1–47:12
12. Joseph during the famine	47:13-26
13. Ephraim and Manasseh	47:27–48:22
14. The blessing of Jacob	49:1-28
15. The death of Jacob	49:29–50: 14
16. The death of Joseph	50:15-26

JOSEPH'S "COAT OF MANY COLORS"

One thing Joseph is remembered for is his coat of "many colors."

"Now Israel [Jacob] loved Joseph more than any of his other sons, because he had been born to him in his old age; and he made a richly ornamented robe for him." *37:3*

How you think of this coat or robe is determined on an interpretation of this Hebrew word, which only appears here.

a. The King James Version says, "he made him a coat of many colors."

b. Some scholars think this description applies to the sleeves, so the Revised Standard Version translates it, "he made him a long robe with sleeves."

54

c. Other scholars think that the Hebrew applies to the whole coat, so the New International version states, "he made him a richly ornamented robe for him."

Joseph's deliberate favoritism was clear for all to see: the robe Jacob gave Joseph was ostentatious.

TWO GIANT BIBLE STUDIES
Two comparisons
1. The life of Joseph compared with the experiences of the children of Israel

The author of Genesis knew all about the events described in the book of Exodus and shows in Genesis how the events in the lives of the patriarchs foreshadow the events of Exodus.

Joseph	The children of Israel
1. God's blessing, initially	God's blessing from the start
2. Rises to position of honor	Received with honor in Egypt
3. Thrown into prison, unjustly	Subjected to cruel slavery
4. Only crime: moral integrity	Only crime: evidently blessed by God
5. Elevated as leader of the Egyptians, Joseph held their lives in his hands	Raised up by God, the Egyptians saw that God held these people in his hands.

2. The life of Joseph compared with the life of Daniel

Joseph and Daniel are two of the most godly and faithful men in the Old Testament.

1. Both were captured in their youth:
   • both were model young men
   • both served in a king's court
2. Both were framed and suffered as a result their hardships became a ladder for future success and honor which came as a result of interpreting dreams
3. Both were elevated to the highest positions of office in foreign lands
4. Both lived pure lives
5. Both died in foreign lands.

LIFE OF JOSEPH (B)

📖 **READ FROM GENESIS**
39:1–41:57

MINI BIBLE STUDY
Dreams in the Old Testament

God sometimes used dreams in the Old Testament to reveal his will.

- Genesis 28:12; 31:10-11; 37:5-9; 40:5; 41:1
- Numbers 12:6
- Judges 7:13
- 1 Kings 3:5
- Daniel 2:3; 4:5; 7:1

DREAMS IN THE LIFE OF JOSEPH

Each time there were dreams featured in Joseph's life it was for his eventual benefit.

- Joseph's two dreams when a teenager: *37:5-11*
- The dreams of the cup bearer and baker: *40:4-23*
- Pharaoh's dream: *41:1-40*

ANOTHER JOSEPH AND HIS DREAMS

In the first two chapters of Matthew's Gospel the phrase, "in a dream" occurs five times.

Matthew 1:20:	"... the Lord appeared to him in a dream and said, '... Do not be afraid to take Mary home as your wife.'"
Matthew 2:12:	"Warned in a dream not to go back to Herod."
Matthew 2:13:	"The angel of the Lord appeared to Joseph in a dream. ... 'Escape to Egypt.'"
Matthew 2:19:	"After Herod died, the angel of the Lord appeared to Joseph in a dream."
Matthew 2:22	"Having been warned in a dream, he withdrew to the district of Galilee."

Now that we have God's revelation in Jesus, there is less need for God to reveal his purpose through dreams. An interesting point to consider.

INTERPRETATION OF DREAMS

Joseph knew that the skill he had in interpreting dreams came from God.

- Only God can interpret dreams accurately.

  "'I cannot do it,' Joseph replied to Pharaoh, 'but God will give Pharaoh the answer [to the dream which nobody else could interpret] he desires.'" *41:16*

  "Then Joseph said to Pharaoh, 'The dreams of Pharaoh are one and the same. God has revealed to Pharaoh what he is about to do.'" *41:25*

  "'It is just as I said to Pharaoh: God has shown Pharaoh what he is about to do.'" *41:28*

- Joseph acts as God's agent, through whom God will make his dreams known. When Joseph was in prison both the baker and cup-bearer had dreams they could not understand.

  "Joseph said to them, 'Do not interpretations belong to God? Tell me your dreams.'" *40:8*

- The people of Israel were a prophetic people through whom God's revelation came to the nations.

LIFE OF JOSEPH (C)

READ FROM GENESIS
42:1–50:26

GOOD CHARACTERISTICS SEEN IN JOSEPH'S LIFE

• Faithful in tough times	39:1-6,20-23
• Resisted temptation	39:7-13
• Wise and faithful in high office	41:14-50
• Showed love towards his brothers	43:30; 45:14
• Acted wisely as he tested his brothers' sincerity	42:6–44:33
• Remained a devoted son	45:23; 47:7
• Trusted God	41:16; 45:8
• Recognized that dreams came from God	41:25-26
• Returned good for evil	50:15-21

In each section of Joseph's life what do you think he learned about God?

THE LORD WAS WITH JOSEPH

In the two lowest points of Joseph's life, he knew God was with him.
- The Lord was with Joseph in Egypt *39:2-3*
- The Lord was with Joseph in prison *39:21*

58

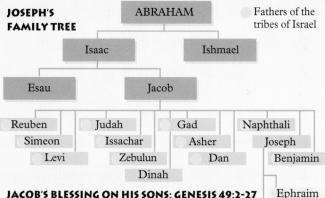

JOSEPH'S FAMILY TREE

ABRAHAM

● Fathers of the tribes of Israel

Isaac — Ishmael

Esau — Jacob

Reuben, Simeon, Levi, Judah, Issachar, Zebulun, Dinah, Gad, Asher, Dan, Naphthali, Joseph, Benjamin

Ephraim, Manasseh

JACOB'S BLESSING ON HIS SONS: GENESIS 49:2-27

This is the longest poem in Genesis, and is known as "The Blessing of Jacob". The blessings were for Jacob's twelve sons and for their descendants.

59

A KEY VERSE

"You intended to harm me, but God intended it for good to accomplish what is now being done, the saving of many lives." *50:20*

STUDY A THEME IN GENESIS
6. GENESIS AND THE BOOK OF REVELATION

GENESIS AND REVELATION COMPARED
- Genesis tells us about the beginning of the world.
- Revelation tells us about the consummation of the world.

GENESIS 1–3 AND REVELATION 21–22
There is a striking contrast between the first three chapters of the Bible and the last three chapters of the Bible.

Genesis 1–3	Topic	Revelation 21–22
"In the beginning God created the heavens and the earth." *1:1*	**1.** Heaven and earth	"Then I saw a new heaven and a new earth." *Revelation 21:1*
"The darkness he called 'night.'" *1:5*	**2.** Night	"There will be no night there." *Revelation 21:25*
"God made two great lights." *1:16*	**3.** Sun and moon	"The city does not need the sun or the moon to shine on it." *Revelation 21:23*
Satan comes to deceive humankind. *3:1*	**4.** Satan	Satan is banished for ever. *Revelation 20:10*
A garden which is defiled. *3:6-7*	**5.** Garden and city	An undefiled city. *Revelation 21:27*
Triumph of serpent. *3:13*	**6.** Triumph	Triumph of the Lamb. *Revelation 22:3*
"I will greatly increase your pains. . ." *3:16*	**7.** Pain	"There will be no more pain." *Revelation 21:4*
"Cursed is the ground because of you." *3:17*	**8.** Curse	"No longer will there be any curse." *Revelation 22:3*
Driven from God's presence. *3:24*	**9.** God's presence	"Now the dwelling of God is with men." *Revelation 21:3*

SIMILARITIES BETWEEN GENESIS AND REVELATION
• The Bible opens with humankind ruined and paradise lost.
• The plan of salvation is set in operation in Genesis 3:15.
• The Bible closes with humankind redeemed and paradise regained.

THE START OF GENESIS AND THE END OF REVELATION IN SYMBOLS

(alpha)
CREATION   REDEMPTION   (omega)
NEW CREATION

THE TREE OF LIFE
The Bible starts with a garden in Genesis 2:8 and ends with a garden in Revelation 22:1-2.

MINI BIBLE STUDY
See what other comparisons and contrasts you find in Genesis 1–2 and Revelation 21–22.

STUDY A THEME IN GENESIS
7. NAMES AND NUMBERS

NAMES OF GOD IN GENESIS

In the Bible, names are extremely important. They reveal the identity of the person.

We will not know God fully until we see him in heaven, but in the meantime one of the ways he has revealed who he is, is by the names used to describe him.

It is informative to discover the many different names for God used by the writer of Genesis. Each name is used in an appropriate way within the context of writing.

ELOHIM

The Hebrew word for God is *"Elohim"*.
• Elohim is the Creator   *1:1*
• Elohim is the Redeemer   *2:7-15; 3:8-15, 21*

NAMES AND TITLES USED FOR GOD

Hebrew name	Meaning	Significance	Reference in Genesis
1. El-Elyon	Most High	God is sovereign, the maker of heaven and earth	*14:18*
2. Shapat	Judge	The Righteous God	*18:25*
3. El Olam	The eternal God	The One who exists forever	*21:33*
4. Yahweh-jireh	The Lord provides	God meets our needs	*22:13-14*
5. El Shaddai	God of mountains	God is all-powerful	*17:1-5*
6. El Elohe-Yisrael	The God of Israel	The God who cares for his people	*33:20; 34:6*

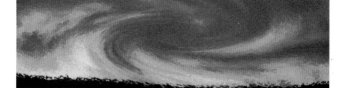

WHAT ABOUT "JEHOVAH" AND "YAHWEH ?

The word "Jehovah" does not appear in Hebrew. The personal name for God, which God revealed to Moses is "Yahweh". It means, "The One who is always present". This word was so holy that the Israelites never said it aloud. To remind them, they wrote the consonants YHWH (for Yahweh), and the vowels of Adonai, which means "Lord". When they spoke of God they said, "Adonai", meaning Lord.

YHWH + ADONAI = JEHOVAH

- From "YHWH" translators took the letter Y,
  (which was often read as "J'),   **J**
- with the first vowel of Adonai (which was often read as "e").   **E**
- They took the second consonant from "YHWH", "H",   **H**
- with the second vowel from Adonai, "O".   **O**
- They took the third consonant from "YHWH", "W",
  (often read as "V"),   **V**
- with the third vowel from Adonai, "a."   **A**
- Finally, they took the last consonant from "YHWH" "H."   **H**

So the resulting hybrid word is "Jehovah." Some translations now use Yahweh. Others translations insert LORD, using small capitals.

63

NUMBERS WITH SYMBOLIC SIGNIFICANCE IN GENESIS

The number "7"
The number "7" in scripture is linked to perfection, completeness and fulfilment.
- The opening verse of Genesis, in Hebrew, consists of 7 words.
- The second verse of Genesis, in Hebrew, consists of 14 words (7x2=14).
- There are 7 days of creation.
- There are various sevens in the flood narrative.
- There are 70 (7x10=70) descendants of Noah's sons in chapter 10.
- Abraham is given a sevenfold promise in *12:2-3*.

- 7 years of abundance are followed by seven years of famine in Egypt in chapter *41*.
- Jacob has 70 descendants in chapter *46*.

The number "12"
The number "12" in the Bible is linked to God's choosing his people and electing individuals.
- Israel had 12 sons, *35:22-27; 42:13, 32*.
- Israel, the people of God, comprised 12 tribes, *49:28*.

KEY VERSES TO MEMORIZE
FROM GENESIS

HIDING GOD'S WORD IN OUR HEARTS

The psalmist gives many reasons for hiding God's Word in our hearts and minds. The reason he gives in Psalm 119:11 may be one that we rarely reflect on:

"I have hidden your word in my heart that I might not sin against you.

KEY VERSES FROM GENESIS

1. "In the beginning God created the heavens and the earth." *1:1*
2. "And I will put enmity between you and the woman, and between your offspring and hers; he will crush your head, and you will strike his heel." *3.15*
3. "Abraham believed the Lord, and he credited it to him as righteousness." *15:6*
4. "I am with you and will watch over you wherever you go ..." *28:15*
5. "You intended to harm me, but God intended it for good to accomplish what is now being done, the saving of many lives." *50:20*